FIRST DISCOVERY LOOK·AND·LEARN BOOKS

On the Farm

Illustrations by Henri Galeron

Cartwheel Books®
SCHOLASTIC INC.
New York Toronto London Auckland Sydney
Mexico City New Delhi Hong Kong Buenos Aires

All kinds of birds live on the farm.
Some farms have roosters, hens,
geese, turkeys, peacocks,
and fluffy baby chicks.

There's a duck pond on this farm.
All kinds of ducks swim in the pond.
Their webbed feet help them
move quickly through the water.

Cows and bulls roam outdoors
on the farm.
During the winter months,
they live in a barn.
The cows are milked twice a day.
Rabbits are raised in a large cage
called a hutch.

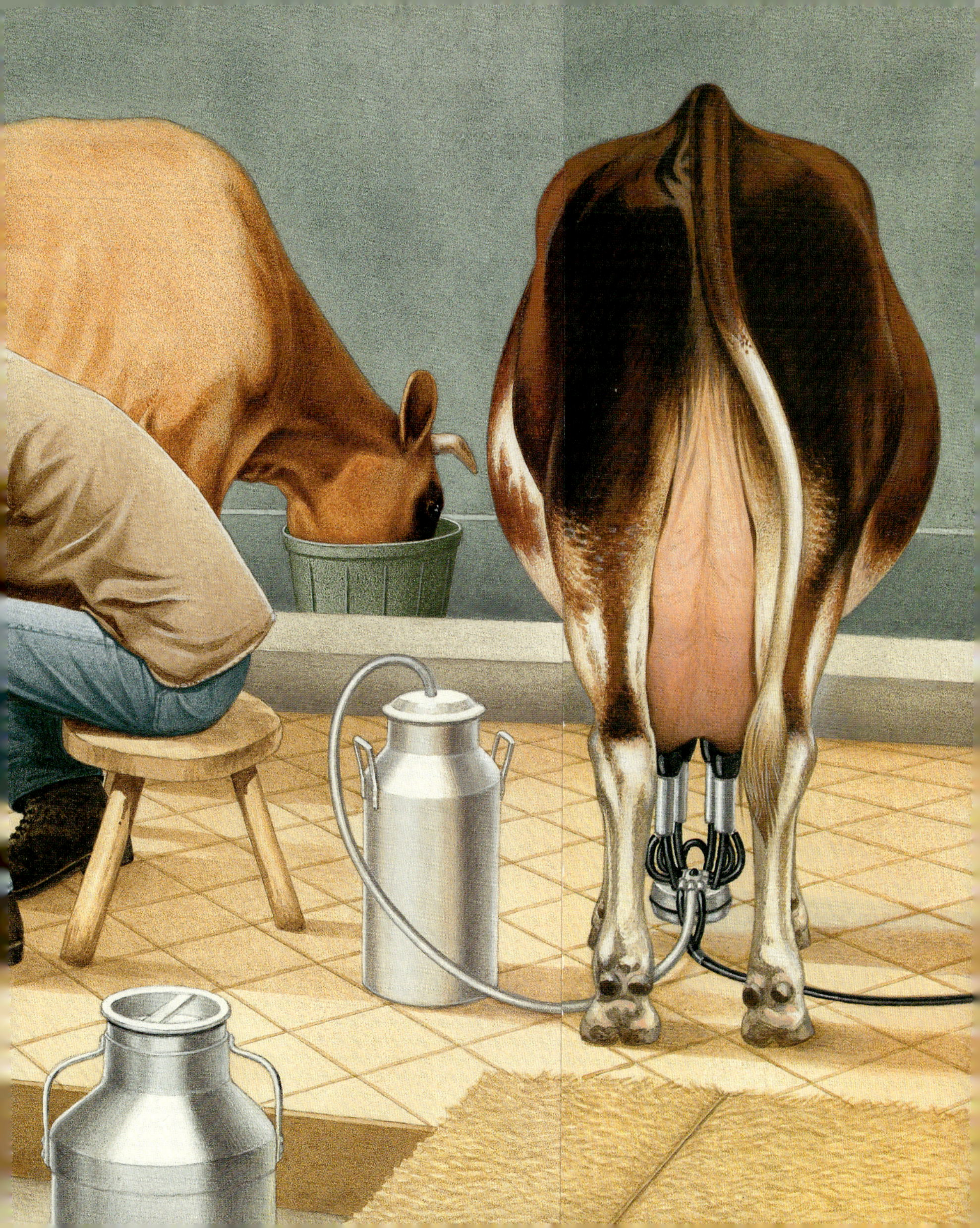

Pigs live in a pen.
This is where they eat, drink, sleep,
and play in the mud.

In spring and summer, sheep roam outdoors in the pasture. When their wool is sheared, or trimmed, it keeps them cool. Come autumn, the sheep are taken to the pen where they spend the winter.

Many tools and machines are needed to keep the farm running smoothly.

These animals graze on fresh grass
in the pasture all day long.
Some eat weeds and wildflowers, too.

In addition to raising
many animals on the far
farmers also grow
many fruits and vegetabl

henho
chicken ya
sheep barn
sheep pen
farmhouse
vegetable garden

This is a picture of the entire farm.
Can you find the different homes
of all the farm animals?

Look carefully and you will see all the anima

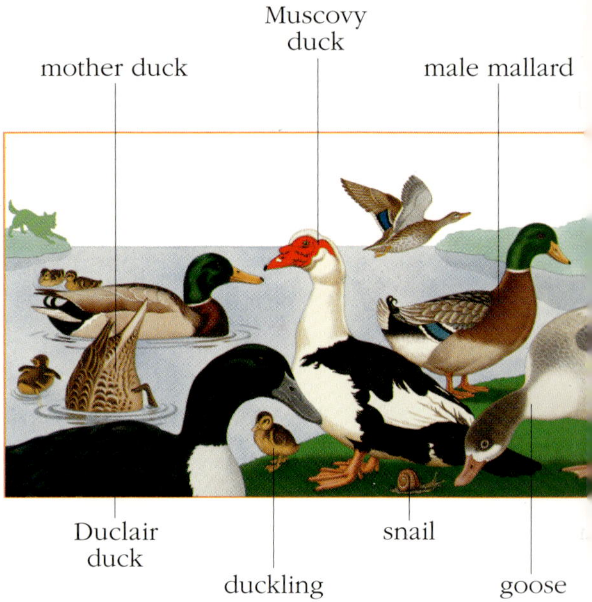

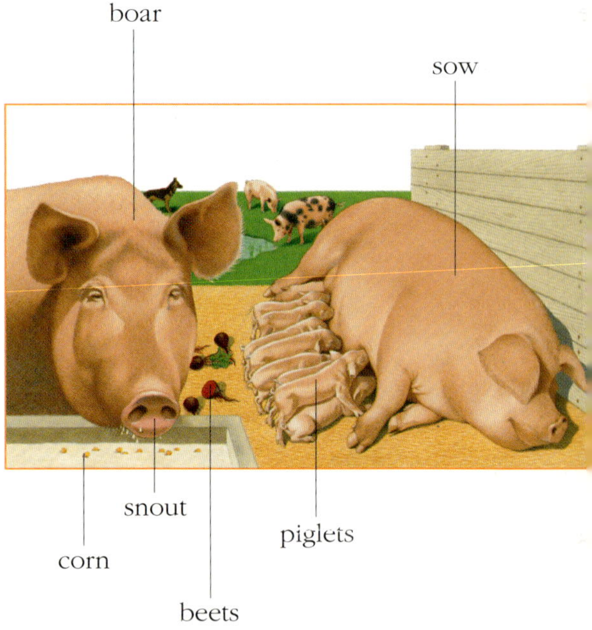